Blessings
Through Time

MM Myers

Published by Hemingway Publishers

Cover design by Hemingway Publishers

ISBN: Printed in the United States

HEMINGWAY
PUBLISHERS

Dedication

For all my kids and grands this one is especially dedicated to Faith, you are an amazing young lady, and I'm truly honored and blessed to call you granddaughter.

Acknowledgment

Above all thank you Jesus, my family and friends that have encouraged me to write. My husband and our son's and their families, also Cece Johnson, Helen Crow, and I cannot forget Faith Fleming for all your hard work to help me get this story out love you all so much. I also would like to express my appreciation to all the individuals whose names may not be mentioned here but have played a part in inspiring me. Thank you all for your love, and encouragement.

CONTENTS

About the Author

Mary Myers is a natural-born storyteller who has captivated her children and grandchildren for years with her imaginative tales. Though putting pen to paper has been a challenge, Mary has persevered in her dream of sharing her stories with the world. With the help of technology and the encouragement of her supportive family, Mary has embarked on a new chapter as a published author. Her heartfelt stories, infused with gratitude and a abiding faith, offer readers a glimpse into the rich inner life of this passionate and enthusiastic storyteller. Mary's journey from reluctant writer to published author is a testament to the power of determination and the gift of a vibrant, creative mind.

Disclaimer

This is a work of fiction. Unless otherwise indicated, all the names, characters, businesses, places, events and incidents in this book are either the product of the author's imagination or used in a fictitious manner. Any resemblance to actual persons, living or dead, or actual events is purely coincidental.

Dolly

If I were given a doll with such a rich history and connection to Mary, the mother of Jesus, I would feel truly honored and blessed. It would be a cherished heirloom.

As I prepared for bed, listening and imagining the precious moments Mary and Jesus spent together, I felt a deep sense of gratitude for being entrusted with such a precious artifact.

The stories of my family's history, intertwined with the doll's lineage, would provide me with a profound sense of identity and belonging. It would remind me of the importance of faith, love, and the enduring power of God's grace throughout the generations.

Introduction

Each night, as my parents closed the door and the soft glow of lamplight enveloped my room, I would hold the doll close. Feeling a connection to Mary and Jesus, and all the others that held this sweet baby doll before me...

As my parents tucked me into bed, I felt the weight of the doll as I held her close. Her appearance reminded me of Mary, the mother of Jesus. It had been handed down for generations.

"Good night," my parents waved as they closed the bedroom door.

This doll passed down through the generations, would serve as a tangible reminder of the living hope we have in Jesus Christ. It would symbolize the enduring faith of my ancestors and inspire me to cultivate a deep relationship with God, just as Mary did.

"Let the doll remind you of the hope we have in Jesus," my mother said when it was handed down to me.

"How will this doll do that?" I remembered asking.

She chuckled, "That's for you to find out, but I can say that this could inspire a deeper relationship."

With each passing day, I would strive to live a life worthy of this precious gift, seeking to emulate the love, compassion, and faith that Mary and Jesus exemplified. I would hold onto the stories shared by my parents, treasuring the wisdom and lessons they imparted.

Chapter 1.

The Special Doll

I had just finished brushing my long brown hair and was pulling back the blankets on my bed, when Mama called me to the living room. "We have a gift for you, dear," she said, smiling. Daddy held out a small wooden old cloth doll dressed in blue with some kind of yarn hair.

"This belonged to your Grandma, and she wanted you to have it," Daddy explained to Faith. I took the doll gently in my hands, peering at its worn face. Mama began to share the doll's awe inspiring history. "Great Grandma received it from her mother, who heard the story from her mother before that. They said this very doll was crafted by Mary, Jesus's mother, as a toy for him when he was but just a baby boy!" Then Jesus and his earthly father Joseph, since they were carpenters, made it even more special.

I gasped at the idea of holding something so old yet well-loved over the centuries. Mama went on, "After Jesus grew, the doll was passed down through generations of different families. It brought comfort to children at all times through generations. And now, it will watch over you as you sleep."

That night, I curled up in bed with the doll tucked in my

arms. "Goodnight, Mary doll," I whispered. Before drifting off, I wondered - did Jesus himself play with this very toy? Did his mother, Mary, hold it and tell him bedtime stories, just as my parents did for me? I fell asleep dreaming of biblical days gone by and of the doll's journey that led it all the way to me.

But how did they know it had belonged to Jesus, the son of God? Soon, she would learn so much... but not tonight. Tonight was sleep....

Chapter 2.

A Gift From Heaven

As Faith drifts off to sleep, clutching me (Dolly) close, I feel stirred to share a piece of my long history. My clothes and body are worn from years of little hands holding tight, but my spirit remains.

"I remember the day Mary crafted me from scraps of fabric, stitching with careful love," I whisper into the night. "Jesus, still a babe, was her light and joy. 'This doll will be his companion,' said Mary to Joseph. And so I was given as a gift to the child who would grow to save humankind."

"Jesus laughed with childish glee to receive me as his own. Our days were spent playing in the meadows and hills, Jesus talking to me of all he saw through youthful eyes. I witnessed miracles even then, in the small ways he showed kindness. In the evening, Mary would find us, and Jesus would cradle me as she sang lullabies."

"Many hands I've known since, but the blessings of my beginning have stayed with this soul of cloth, wood, and stuffing. I am blessed to be here now, watching over another dear one, as I once did the Son of God himself oh so very long ago."

The child's eyes flutter at my tale, dreaming of faraway places and people I've known. I wish this sweet child rest, as Mary did for Jesus long ago in the past.

Chapter 3.

The Purple Wildflower

"Let me tell you about a special day I spent with Jesus, from my earliest memories," the doll began in a soft, whispery voice.

"It was a sunny afternoon, and Jesus was about five years old. He picked me up and said, 'Come, my friend, I want to show you something.' We walked out to the hills behind our home. When we reached the top, Jesus sat down and gazed out at the countryside.

"The land was dry and dusty then, as people struggled in poverty. But Jesus wasn't sad - he smiled at the tiny purple wildflowers that had managed to bloom despite the harsh ground. 'Look how beautiful they are,' he said. 'Their color makes me happy, like how God's love makes me happy inside."

"Then something amazing happened. Jesus gently picked a flower and held it out in his palm. Before my button eyes, the dried soil in his hand grew dark and moist. The flower's petals perked up and its stem lengthened, until it had doubled in size! Jesus turned to me, eyes shining. 'Now it can help bring more smiles," he said.

"From that day on, I knew Jesus had a power like no other. But more than anything, I saw how kind and caring he was, even as a boy. He had so much love to share with the world. And I was blessed to know him, travel with him, just as you are blessed now by this story."

The child's eyes were wide with wonder at the doll's unique memory of Jesus so long ago.

Chapter 4.

Whispers From Yesteryear

"Did you ever get dirty?" asked Faith. The doll nodded gently. "Yes, I indeed got my fair share of dirt and tears in those days," she said with a soft chuckle. "Jesus was always exploring and learning, dragging me along on his adventures! There was the time we went down to the river, and I fell in the mud. And another I got caught on a bush during one of our hillside talks.

"But Mary never scolded, only smiled at her curious boy. 'Accidents will happen with such an active spirit,'" she'd say as she mended my seams. Her touch was always deft and caring. I'd be good as new in no time, ready to listen to Jesus's wonderings once more.

"He did like to bring me along wherever he went, even into town to listen at his father Joseph's carpentry shop. But some of my fondest memories are of accompanying Jesus to the synagogue on Sabbath days. I'd peer from his arms as he watched and listened intently to the rabbis discuss the scriptures.

"Even at a young age, Jesus had such a thirst for knowledge and such compassion for people. I felt blessed to be his companion and witness to who he was growing to become. It was the greatest honor for this simple doll."

The child's eyes shone with interest at the doll's recollections of Jesus's early life. What a treasure to hold stories from so long ago!

Chapter 5.

A Doll's View of History

The doll settled in comfortably as Faith's eyes began to droop sleepily. "I have one more tale to share of my time with Jesus if you'd like to hear it before resting," she offered gently. The child nodded, cozy under the blankets.

"It was many years later when Jesus had begun his important work," the doll began. "Word had spread of his powerful words and healings. One afternoon, a huge crowd had gathered on a hillside to hear him speak. Jesus held me tenderly as he looked out at all the faces, filled with such care and wisdom beyond his years.

"Then he began to teach. I'd never heard anything like it - the parables of seeds and soils, the Sermon on the Mount, lessons of faith, hope, and love. The people listened in awe. Jesus had a way of explaining God's messages simply so all could understand. As the sun sank low, no one wanted to leave his side.

"But I think my favorite part was seeing the joy light Jesus's face as he helped people. A man in pain, a child without hope - with a touch and compassionate words, their burdens would be lifted. Jesus was fulfilling his purpose to bring light to the world, even through a little doll's observation. I felt so lucky to be his friend and to have been at his side during that amazing day in history."

Faith's little eyes drifted closed, lulled by the story. The doll recalled many years earlier Mary tucking in Jesus when he was but a child... oh such sweet memories. And memories she held on to for each new child dolly was given to. One child at a time, she was reliving her many years with each child person she'd watched grow up... oh how Dolly had loved every one of her many children, but her favorite will always be Jesus, her first child and yet a savior for all humanity.

Chapter 6.

A Carpenter's Touch

The doll smiled gently as the child nestled in for the night…"While Mary created me originally from cloth, it was indeed Jesus who gave me new life through his carpentry skills.

"I remember lying on the workshop table as Jesus studied my seams and joints. 'Mother made you well, but let me see if I can improve your form,' he said to me. Just as Joseph taught him, Jesus's hands were deft and precise as he carefully removed my cloth parts and fashioned new limbs from wood.

"Each scrape and sanding was done with such focus and care. I could see Jesus's love for his craft blossoming, even in such small tasks. When at last I was reconstructed, it was as if I had been reborn - more substantial and more lasting to accompany children for years to come.

"But the most special moment was yet to come. With the smallest chisel, Jesus carved out a place in my chest and placed within it a heart of wood. 'Now you can keep my memories and all those whose lives you touch,' he whispered with a smile. And from that day on, this heart has done just that."

Faith's eyes fluttered shut, lulled by the doll's tale of Jesus's gift that has endured through centuries.

Chapter 7.

Childhood Years

Dolly smiled softly at Faith's question. "Jesus had a very loving relationship with both Mary and Joseph," she began.

"Mary doted on her son and was so proud of his curious spirit and kind heart. Even as a young boy, Jesus had a special closeness and respect for his mother. I have many memories of seeing them working together in the home or Mary brushing Jesus's hair as he told her about his day.

"Joseph was also devoted to Jesus, teaching him the carpentry trade from a young age. Jesus was an eager student and tried his best to help his family. I could see how much Jesus looked up to Joseph as a father figure.

"They lived simply but with great faith. Jesus always did chores and listened well, though he did have his moments, too!" Dolly chuckled. "Like any child, he loved to explore. But he knew how blessed he was to have parents who loved and guided him."

"All in all, it was a very caring home. I was lucky to witness the strong bond between Jesus, Mary, and Joseph during his childhood years in Nazareth." Faith smiled, picturing the happy family scenes.

Chapter 8.

Disciples

Faith's eyes shone with curiosity. "Tell me, what was it like to witness Jesus teaching others?" she asked Dolly eagerly.

Dolly thought back fondly. "Even from a young age, Jesus had such a gift for sharing knowledge in a way anyone could understand," she began. Oh, and he truly loved everyone, but his favorite was the children. He even let them hold me as they gathered around to hear him. And children gathered around Jesus like moths to a flame.

"When he was just a boy, I remember him explaining scriptures so clearly to Mary during their chats. His neighbors, too, would gather to listen as Jesus opened their eyes to God's messages of love.

"But nothing compared to hearing him teaching as an adult. Jesus spoke with such passion, wisdom, and compassion. When he taught in the synagogues or on the hillsides, you could have heard a pin drop - no one wanted to miss a word!

"Yet Jesus had a way of making even the darkest truths feel accessible. Through his parables and stories, truths that had been obscured for so long were brought into the light. It was like he could

17

see into every person's heart.

"Just being in his presence left you feeling uplifted, hopeful, and ready to spread more kindness in the world. I was blessed to witness Jesus sharing the greatest lessons of all - of love, forgiveness, and service to others."

Faith sighed happily, picturing that beautiful sight. What an honor it must have been!

Chapter 9.

Building God's Kingdom

Dolly thought carefully about Faith's question.

"From what I know based on Jesus's conversations, he chose the 12 people who would become his closest disciples very intentionally," Dolly began.

"It started when Jesus began traveling around Galilee, spreading his message of God's love and mercy. Naturally, some were more drawn to his teachings than others. A group of men in particular - Peter, Andrew, James and John - seemed especially captivated by Jesus after hearing one of his sermons by the sea.

"These men became Jesus's first disciples. He saw their willingness to learn, to serve others, and to spread hope to those in need. From there, Jesus's reputation grew, and more began following in hopes of healing or guidance.

"Jesus knew he needed helpers to continue his work after he returned to heaven. So, he selected 12 extraordinary men to devote themselves fully as apostles. Through signs or intimate moments, Jesus discerned each man's character, strengths, and calling.

"In the end, he chose a diverse group - fishermen, tax collectors, others. But all had heard Jesus's message clearly and committed to living it out each day, no matter the hardships. Together, they formed the foundation to build God's kingdom on earth."

Faith listened, enraptured by this glimpse into how Jesus recruited the original 12 apostles. What an amazing time it must have been.

Chapter 10.

Faith's Journey with Jesus

Faith loved going to bed. Getting to hear about Jesus was a wonderful bonus, especially for someone who was there. Well, she was someone special, too, right, even if she was a Dolly. Dolly was there. Jesus took her with him on his walks his trips, but how did her grandma end up with this very special dolly? Maybe one day she'd find out right now she was enjoying these stories. She wondered what her story would be tonight! That night, before Dolly told her another story, Faith started running a fever. Her parents had been reading her their nightly story. She hadn't felt bad now, but not right all day. Her mom had kissed her on the head and said, "Faith, honey, I think you are running a fever I'll be back in a min."

Faith only closed her eyes for a moment and mom was back to check her temp 101.5. She waited a little bit and took her temp again, hoping she was wrong 102.9, wow, it's going up fast.

She asked Faith, "Honey, are you hurting anywhere?"

Faith was out again. Mommy took her temp again, 103.2. She went and got some children's meds she'd had on hand and a spoon. She was back in just a couple of minutes. She asked Kenny, Faith's daddy, how is she doing?

Kenny, Faith's father, was very concerned. They not only gave Faith the medication, but Kenny and Nicole prayed for their little Faith. Faith could hear them, but they seemed so far away…

She dreamed she was walking on a beach and then there was this man. "I know you," she said…

"You do," he said …

"Yes," said Faith. "I have your Dolly, you are Jesus."

"Well, now that you are right. How did you know?" asked Jesus. "Because I know," said Faith.

"Jesus I'm running a fever. I heard my parents praying for me."

"Yes," Jesus said.

"You will be fine, but for now, you are going to spend some time with me. Is that ok with you?" asked Jesus.

"Oh yes," said Faith. She could not believe her luck. So that night, even though she was in her own bed running a pretty high fever she was with Jesus at the beach watching boats so since she was here, she talked to him

Faith smiled up at Jesus, feeling a sense of peace and comfort wash over her. "Jesus, can I ask you a question?" she said, her voice filled with curiosity.

"Of course, my child," Jesus replied, his eyes filled with warmth and love.

Faith took a moment to gather her thoughts. "Jesus, how did my grandma end up with this special dolly that belonged to you? Did you give it to her?"

Jesus smiled, his eyes twinkling. "Your grandma was a woman of great faith and love, just like you, Faith. She lived her life in service to others, spreading kindness and sharing the message of love that I taught. One day, long, long ago, when your great great great grandma was in a small village, she stumbled upon a humble wooden box in a shop. Inside, she saw the most beautiful dolls, each one crafted with love and care."

Faith's eyes widened with anticipation, eager to hear the rest of the story.

"Among those dolls, there was one that caught her eye," Jesus continued. "It was the dolly, the one you now hold dear. Your grandma felt a deep connection to that doll as if it carried a special presence. She knew in her heart that it was meant for her."

Faith held the dolly closer, feeling a sense of wonder and gratitude. "But how did the dolly come to be, Jesus? Who made it?"

"Don't you know," Jesus smiled gently and said, "The dolly was made by a humble carpenter, a man who poured his love and craftsmanship into each creation. He had a special gift for infusing his work with a touch of divine energy. When he made the dolly, he dedicated it to me to carry my presence and love wherever it went."

Jesus nodded, his eyes filled with love. "Indeed, my child. The dolly carries a small piece of my essence, a reminder of the love and guidance I offer to all who hold it close. It is a symbol of faith, hope, and the everlasting love that surrounds you."

Faith hugged the dolly tightly, feeling a deep sense of connection to Jesus. She knew that even in her fevered state, she was in the presence of something truly special. As she drifted off to sleep, she held onto the dolly, knowing that Jesus was watching over her, guiding her through the night.

Faith hugged the dolly tightly, feeling a deep sense of connection to Jesus. She knew that even in her fevered state, she was in the presence of something truly special. As she drifted off to sleep, she held onto the dolly, knowing that Jesus was watching over her, guiding her through the night.

She could hear her parents as they contacted 911 to ask if she would be ok. They worried and prayed. The ambulance rushed, and here the paramedics came in and took her to the hospital. She was so feverish even doctors weren't sure what was going to happen, but Jesus did, and he stayed with faith, never leaving her side.

Jesus told Faith that everyone had pain and suffering on this earth ever since the fall. Faith asked, "Will you help me to understand Jesus?"

"Yes, my child," he said.

Jesus explains the fall of man and why we are given free will Jesus sat by Faith's side in the hospital room, his eyes filled with compassion as she asked her question after question He took a deep breath, preparing to explain the fall of man and the concept of free will.

Long ago, in the beginning of creation, God made a perfect world," Jesus began. "He created Adam and Eve, the first humans, and placed them in a beautiful garden called Eden. They had everything they needed and enjoyed a close and harmonious relationship with God."

Faith listened intently, her eyes locked on Jesus's face, eager to understand.

"However, God also gave Adam and Eve something very precious - the gift of free will," Jesus continued. "He wanted them to have the ability to make choices, to love and obey Him willingly. But with this gift came the possibility of using their free will to go against God's will."

Faith's brow furrowed in confusion. "But why would they do that, Jesus? If everything was perfect, why would they choose to disobey God?"

Jesus nodded, understanding the complexity of the question. "You see, Faith, Adam, and Eve were tempted by the serpent, who convinced them that by eating from the tree of the knowledge of good and evil, they would become like God. It was a temptation to seek knowledge and power beyond what God had intended for them."

Faith's eyes widened with realization. "So, they ate from the tree, even though God had told them not to?"

Jesus nodded sadly. "Yes, my child. Adam and Eve made the choice to go against God's command, and in doing so, they brought sin and brokenness into the world. Their act of disobedience is what we refer to as the 'fall of man.' It separated humanity from God's perfect presence and introduced pain, suffering, and the consequences of sin into the world."

Faith's heart felt heavy as she absorbed the weight of this truth. "But Jesus, why didn't God just take away their free will? Wouldn't that have prevented all of this?"

Jesus smiled gently, a glimmer of understanding in his eyes. "God's love for us is so immense, Faith. He desires our love and obedience to be genuine and freely chosen. Taking away our free will would have made us mere puppets, incapable of truly experiencing the depth of love and connection that comes from choosing Him willingly."

He reached out and gently held Faith's hand. "But even in the midst of the consequences of the fall, God had a plan to redeem humanity. He sent me, his son, to restore the broken relationship between God and mankind through my life, death, and resurrection. I came to offer forgiveness, salvation, and the promise of eternal life to all who believe in me."

Faith's eyes filled with hope, her heart filled with gratitude. "Thank you, Jesus, for explaining it to me. Even though it's hard to understand, I trust that God's plan is perfect, and I'm grateful for your sacrifice."

Jesus smiled, his love radiating from him. "You are wise beyond your years, Faith. Keep seeking understanding and know that I am always with you, guiding you through life's challenges."

As the night wore on, Faith held onto the dolly tightly, finding comfort in knowing that Jesus was by her side, even in the midst of pain and suffering. And with that assurance, she drifted off to sleep, feeling a profound sense of peace and love surrounding her.

As Faith woke up the next morning, her fever had miraculously subsided. She felt a renewed energy coursing through her veins, and her hunger pangs reminded her of the breakfast she had missed.

Excitedly, she tried to tell the doctors and her parents about her encounter with Jesus, eager to share the joy and comfort she had experienced. However, the doctors, although relieved by her improved condition, dismissed her story as a product of her fevered imagination.

But Faith knew in her heart that what she had experienced was real, that she had indeed encountered Jesus in her time of need. There was a sense of confidence within her that she couldn't explain, a deep knowing that went beyond her young age.

Days turned into weeks, and Faith's health continued to improve. She resumed her normal activities, attending school, playing with friends, and spending time with her family. But the memory of her encounter with Jesus remained etched in her heart.

One ordinary Sunday, as Faith sat in the church pew with her family, the pastor read a passage from the Bible. It was the story of Jesus asking his disciples, "Who do you say I am?"

Faith's heart skipped a beat as she remembered the question Jesus had asked her during their encounter. She felt a surge of courage and stood up, raising her hand to get the attention of the pastor.

The pastor, intrigued by Faith's eagerness, nodded and invited her to speak. Faith took a deep breath and confidently proclaimed, "I know who Jesus is! He is the Son of God, the savior of the world!" And he was beside me in the hospital.

The congregation gasped in awe, amazed by the conviction and wisdom in Faith's words. The pastor, moved by her faith, smiled warmly and affirmed her response. "Faith, you have spoken truth. Jesus is indeed the Son of God, who came to save us and offer eternal life."

From that day forward, Faith's story spread throughout the community. People marveled at the young girl who had encountered Jesus and had the courage to share her experience. The doctors, who initially dismissed her story, began to question whether there was more to her encounter than they had initially thought.

This was not the end of the story but only the beginning...

www.ingramcontent.com/pod-product-compliance
Lightning Source LLC
LaVergne TN
LVHW010027070426
835510LV00001B/17